DOT·TO·DOT
in Color

WILDLIFE PARADISE

DOT·TO·DOT
in Color

WILDLIFE
PARADISE

30 challenging designs to improve your mental agility

SHANE MADDEN

METRO BOOKS
New York

METRO BOOKS
New York

An Imprint of Sterling Publishing Co., Inc.
1166 Avenue of the Americas
New York, NY 10036

ISBN 978-1-4351-6442-0

For information about custom editions, special sales, and premium and
corporate purchases, please contact Sterling Special Sales at 800-805-5489
or specialsales@sterlingpublishing.com.

2 4 6 8 10 9 7 5 3 1

www.sterlingpublishing.com

Credits
Publisher: Kerry Enzor
Managing Editor: Julia Shone
Senior Editor: Philippa Wilkinson
Editorial Assistant: Emma Harverson
Designer: Mike Lebihan
Production Manager: Zarni Win

Printed in China by RR Donnelley

Contents

Introducing Dot-to-Dot in Color

Get ready to dive into a world of color with the 30 vivid designs in this collection. Each of the dot-to-dot puzzles in this book has been inspired by the rich tones of the animal kingdom, from the sleek blues of jumping dolphins, to the iridescent shades of the tiny hummingbird and the resplendent hues of tropical tree frogs. Simply unravel the web of numbered points to reveal a stunning artwork. You'll be wowed every time.

Bringing Color into your Day

Dot-to-dot puzzles are a great way to switch off from the distractions and stresses of our 24/7 world. Taking the time to concentrate on an absorbing task can help us achieve a state that positive psychology identifies as "flow." Flow activities enable us to tune out from our day-to-day concerns and become immersed in energized focus on the task we are completing. This taps into a central tenet of mindfulness, that is to say being fully involved in the present moment.

More than this, flow activities are characterized by positive channeling of attention and energy. Completing a challenging task gives us a mental boost and encourages a more positive, go-getting attitude. We can use flow activities to revitalize and refresh our minds, and gear ourselves toward a more proactive mind-set.

Use the 30 puzzles in this collection to set you up with a successful approach for the day, or wind-down with them in the evening. The dot-to-dots can be tackled in sections, or completed in a single sitting—simply fit them into your day to discover a sense of achievement and a calmer, more focused mind.

Join the Dots

Each of the puzzles in this book has over 400 numbered points to untangle. Once you get started, you will find the rhythm, following one point to the next to reveal a dynamic scene from the wildlife world. Before you get started, turn to page 10 for top tips on how to approach these extreme dot-to-dots.

Choose which puzzle to start with by turning to the Dot-to-Dot Index on pages 77–79. A thumbnail of each image will help you take your pick from regal jungle beasts, minute insect masterpieces, and preening feathered friends. Creatures from all over the animal kingdom splash their colors across the pages and are perfect subjects for this lively dot-to-dot treatment. All of the pages are blank on the reverse side, which means you can remove and frame your work when you're done.

How to Use This Book

Before you dive into the colorful world of the dot-to-dots in this collection, read through the following pages for advice on how to use this book and for top tips on completing these fiendish puzzles.

A key for each puzzle shows the order in which the color-coded sections should be completed. Follow this order to ensure no premature crossing out of numbers or dots in other sections. The key also lists how many numbered points there are in each section so you can easily identify when you have completed that color. Read the color order down each column, starting with the left column.

Each colored section starts with number "1." The first point is indicated by a star to identify the beginning for each line.

The reverse of each page has been left blank so that you can remove your finished puzzle and display if you wish. However, some reverse pages have color keys. Check the back of each design before removing as you may need the key to complete the next puzzle in the book.

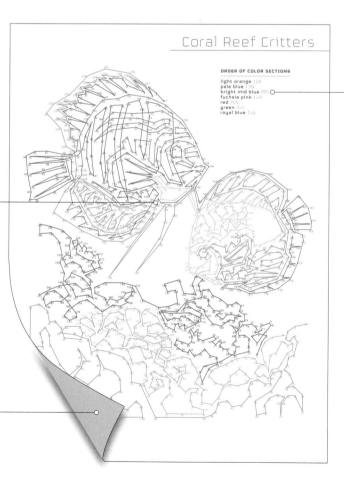

Coral Reef Critters

ORDER OF COLOR SECTIONS

light orange 128
pale blue 109
bright mid blue 201
fuchsia pink 118
red 355
green 245
royal blue 146

Match your colors to those listed in the key for each section. You have the freedom within each color to decide your own tones or shades should you wish.

Turn to pages 77–79 to find finished thumbnails for each of the puzzles in this book. You can use this index to help select which scene from the animal kingdom you would like to try next, or if you need some guidance to complete the puzzle.

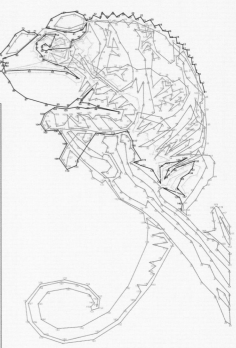

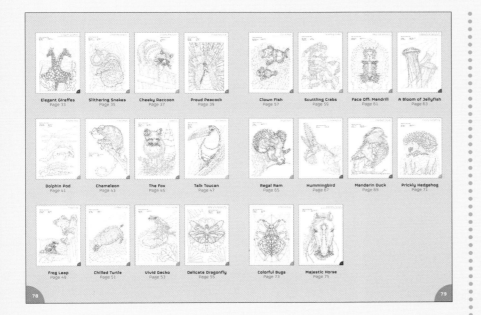

CHOOSING YOUR TOOLS

To complete the puzzles accurately, it is best to use a fine-nibbed felt-tip or roller ball pen in each of the colors listed in the key. You need to be able to keep your lines sharp and clear in those areas where the dots are close together.

The colors listed in the key provide a palette guideline. You have the freedom within each colour to decide your own tones or shades. Whatever you choose, the finished result will be a highly colored scene from the rainforests reaches, ocean depths, or vast skies. You may wish to take some time testing your chosen pens on a spare sheet of paper before starting the puzzle.

Tackling the Dot-to-Dots

The illustrations in this book have been designed with vivid color palettes to evoke the hues of the natural world. The colored sections generally work from lightest color to darkest. Follow the order listed in the key to ensure the best result.

Each colored section starts with number "1" and progresses chronologically to the end dot. The total number of dots in each section is listed in the key so you can identify when you have completed each section. It makes sense to join all of the dots in one section before progressing to the next, following the order recommended in the key.

Everyone will have their own method for approaching these fiendish puzzles, but below are some tips to help you get started.

1. **Prepare your tools:** We recommended using fine-nibbed pens (see Choosing your Tools, page 9) to complete the dot-to-dots, but you can also use colored pencils. If choosing pencils, make sure that they are sharp before you begin so you can keep your lines fine in detailed areas.

2. **Get comfortable:** You can choose to complete these puzzles wherever you like—on your commute, on a lunch break, or in a café. However, to get the most out of the puzzles it is best to choose a quiet spot where you will not be disturbed so that you can fully focus on the task in hand. Having a flat surface to work on with plenty of space will also help.

3. **Use a ruler:** Some of the points are quite far away from each other, and using a ruler will help to keep your lines sharp in more congested areas.

4. **Take it in order:** Each puzzle has been designed to be completed in a certain color order as denoted by the accompanying key. Follow this order so as to avoid crossing through any numbers before you need to use them.

5. **Don't worry:** Try not to get frustrated if you go wrong. Simply locate the error and go back to the last correct point. You will still have a beautifully colored puzzle when you finish.

6. **Closer look:** In some detailed areas you may wish to use a magnifying glass to help you read the numbers clearly.

7. **Pen bleed:** Each reverse side of the puzzle has been left blank so that you can remove your designs once completed, and also to protect against ink bleeding through the page. If you are concerned about your pens bleeding through the paper, simply place an 8 x12 inch sheet of blank paper behind the puzzle that you are working on.

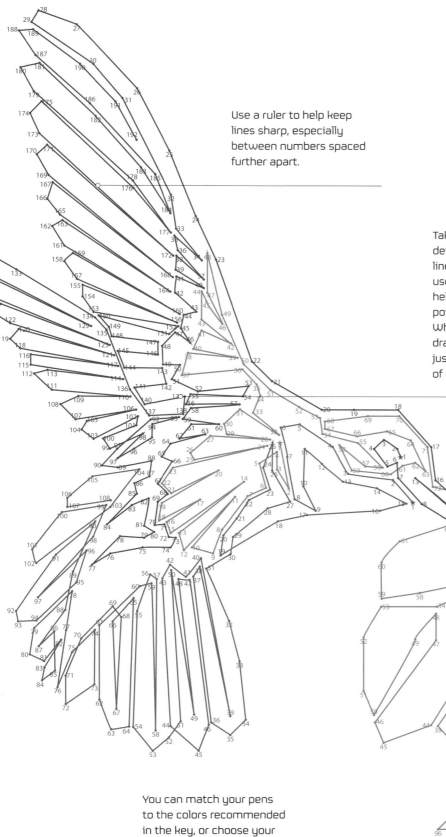

Use a ruler to help keep lines sharp, especially between numbers spaced further apart.

Take care when completing detailed areas to keep your lines crisp. You may wish to use a magnifying glass to help distinguish the numbered points in denser sections. When you step back from the drawing you will find you have just picked out the fine feathers of a wing or a beady eye.

You can match your pens to the colors recommended in the key, or choose your own shades. Follow the order recommended in the key to complete the puzzle.

Creating with Color

Using color has been made easy in this book, with expert color-coded palettes developed for each image to bring the scene strikingly to life—and you can bring your own flair to each drawing by coloring in the completed puzzle.

Coloring Tools

While you need a sharp pencil or fine-nibbed pen to keep your lines crisp when completing the dot-to-dot puzzle, you can choose from a range of options to add color to your image.

Colored pencils are the tool of choice for most coloring in as they can be used to create subtle tonal variations within the image as well as adding fine details. Another option is **watercolor pencils**, which can create a lovely painterly effect; and for a bolder approach, **felt-tip pens** create rich, vibrant images with strong color. You can also experiment with **pastels**, **paints**, and **crayons** to realize a range of different styles. Have fun and explore the different artistic effects you create simply by changing your coloring tools!

Basic Shading Techniques

There are a number of different shading techniques that you can use to add color to your dot-to-dot design, all of which create slightly different effects.

Hatching
Hatching is a series of lines drawn together to give a sense of filled color. The hatching lines can be either straight or curved, and can be drawn close together to give a smooth effect or further apart for a more sketchy look. Hatching is a great way to add color quickly to an image.

Crosshatching
In crosshatching one set of lines overlaps another set. Like hatching, crosshatching can be drawn with the lines close together to create a solid effect or more spaced out with white spaces remaining. For areas of color that you want to appear very smooth, close crosshatching is the best method.

Circular shading
You can also shade with small circles rather than straight lines. Again, you can create denser or more roughly colored areas depending on how close together you keep your lines. This method can be useful for creating texture within your image.

Drawing hatching lines close to and overlapping one another creates a smooth area of color.

When drawn farther apart from one another the hatching lines remain distinct.

Crosshatching when lines are drawn very close together can create a dense solid color.

Spaced further apart, crosshatching lines remain distinct and show areas of white space.

Adding Light and Shade

Create shape and bring depth to each design by adding areas of light and shade. Shading with colored pencils or watercolor pencils is the easiest way to do this. The simplest method is pressure shading, where you place more or less pressure on your pencil to achieve a darker or lighter shade. Alternatively, shade the full area with the lightest shade then go back over areas that you want to make darker, adding extra layers of color to achieve the desired effect.

Shading with pencils can leave flecks of white and show lines between more heavily and less shaded areas. To smooth out the color in your image you can use a colorless blender pencil. Available from most good craft stores, blender pencils can be applied over the top of colored pencils to better merge the different tones.

To intensify shading, you can layer darker colors over basic shading. Layering colors in this way will create a different shade from either of the original colors used and can make for an interesting tonal variation. You can also use different tones within a color range to achieve more depth in your image.

Creating Shape

When adding light and shade to create shape in your image there are three key terms to remember: highlights, shadows, and mid-tones. To create a sense of perspective you will want to add highlights to areas of the image that would be in the sun and shadow in those areas that would be facing away from the light source—mid-tones are those areas in between. You can use the shading techniques above to create these areas of light and shade within your dot-to-dot design.

THE
DOT-TO-DOT
PUZZLES

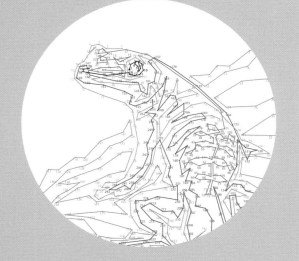

Dawn Chorus

ORDER OF COLOR SECTIONS

orange 76
leaf green 93
light brown 79
coral pink 109

fuchsia pink 154
royal blue 100
burgundy red 98
black 104

Coral Reef Critters

ORDER OF COLOR SECTIONS

light orange 126
pale blue 199
bright mid blue 201
fuchsia pink 118
red 265
green 245
royal blue 146

Lion's Roar

ORDER OF COLOR SECTIONS

golden brown 21
rich brown 540
black 187

Macaws

Macaws

ORDER OF COLOR SECTIONS

light orange 112
bright blue 110
tangerine orange 148
bright red 104
light brown 79
forest green
upper leaf 147;
lower leaf 180;
black 190

23

Crowing Cockerel

ORDER OF COLOR SECTIONS

golden yellow 83	bright red 63
orange 159	burgundy red 50
forest green 324	dark brown 54
royal blue 35	

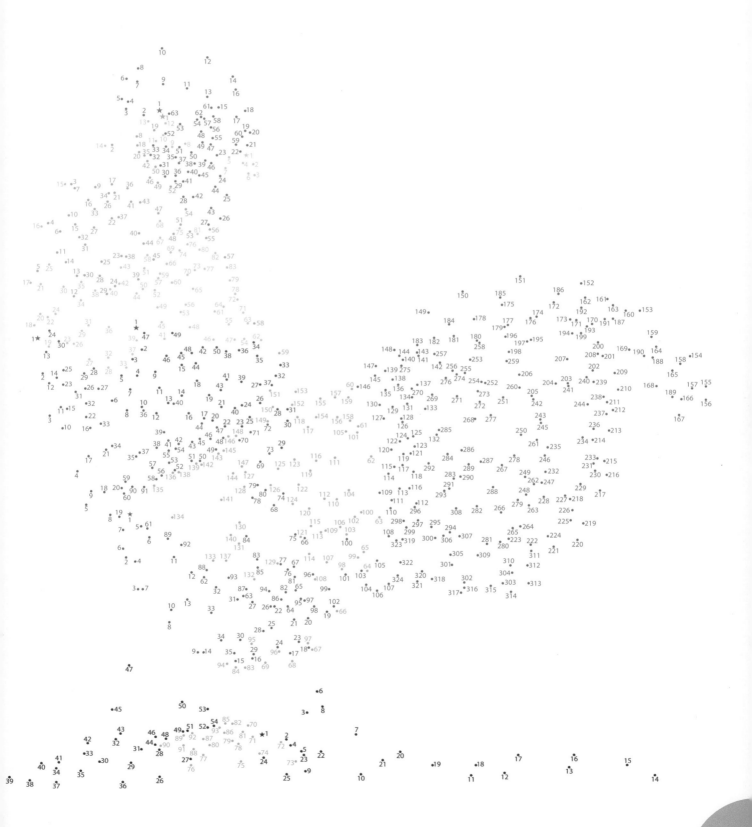

Flutter Butterfly

ORDER OF COLOR SECTIONS

dusty pink 204   light orange 18
duck egg blue 43   tangerine orange 68
green 121   dark blue 296

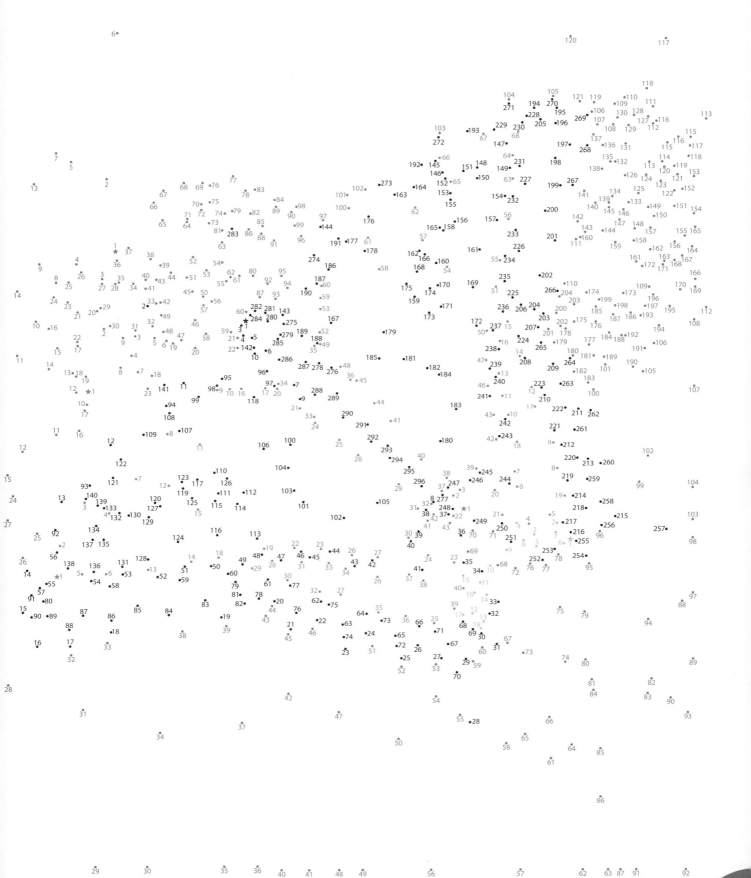

Tiger Stripes

Tiger Stripes

ORDER OF COLOR SECTIONS

lime green 7
golden yellow 106
tangerine orange 214
warm gray 168
grass green 82
black 636

Flamingo Duo

ORDER OF COLOR SECTIONS

pale peach 65   golden yellow 11
soft sea gray 64   fuchsia pink 130
azure sea blue 93   tail feather burgundy 81
sea green 29   pale pink brown 47
orange 8   dark brown 70
tail feather peach 36

Elegant Giraffes

ORDER OF COLOR SECTIONS

Elegant Giraffes

Slithering Snakes

ORDER OF COLOR SECTIONS

pale orange 151
grass green 288
tangerine orange 218
fuchsia pink 209

royal blue 263
violet 38
black 43

Cheeky Raccoon

Cheeky Raccoon

ORDER OF COLOR SECTIONS

warm gray 205
golden orange 219
brown 359
black 180

Proud Peacock

ORDER OF COLOR SECTIONS

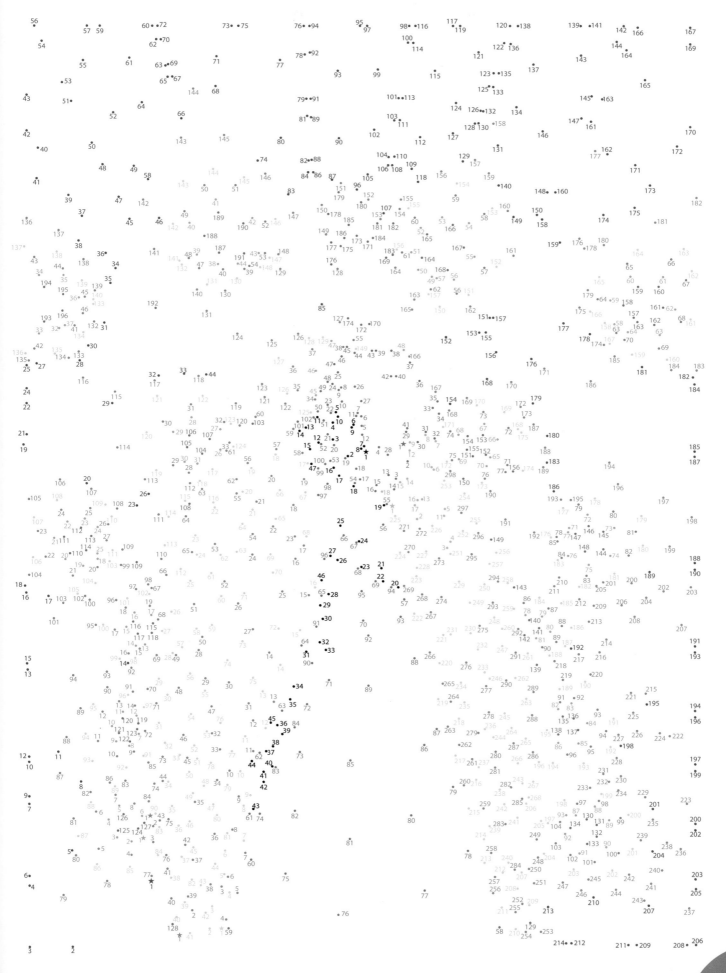

Dolphin Pod

ORDER OF COLOR SECTIONS

golden yellow 130	royal sea blue 87
palest sea blue 55	gray dolphin blue 135
mid sea blue 94	navy dolphin blue 151

Chameleon

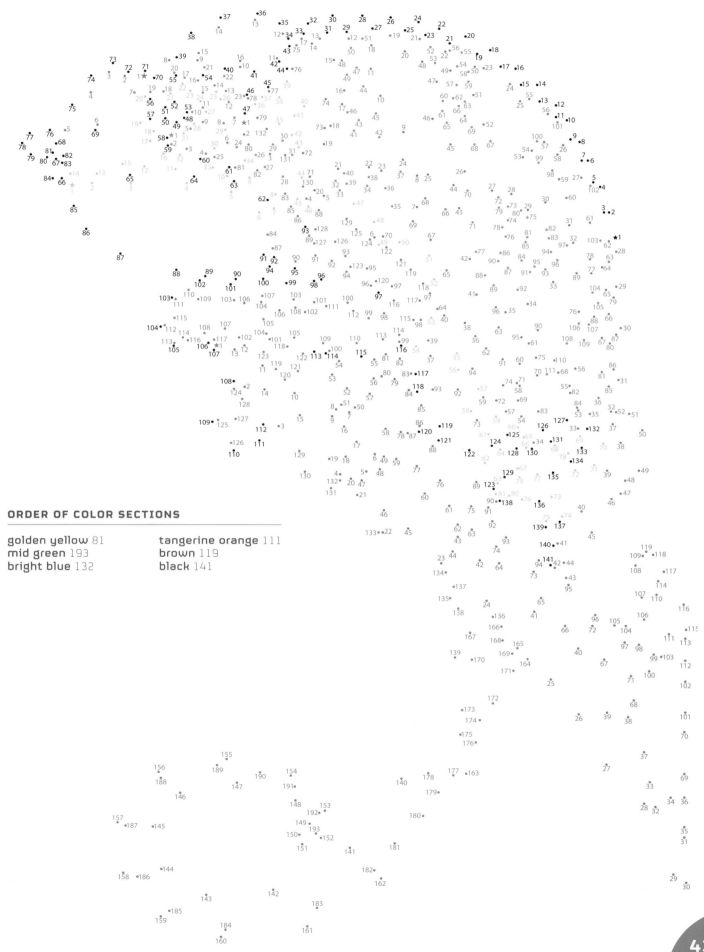

ORDER OF COLOR SECTIONS

golden yellow 81   tangerine orange 111
mid green 193   brown 119
bright blue 132   black 141

The Fox

ORDER OF COLOR SECTIONS

pale brown 237   grass green 142
mushroom brown 53   forest green 52
orange 263   black 196
bright blue 180

Talk Toucan

ORDER OF COLOR SECTIONS

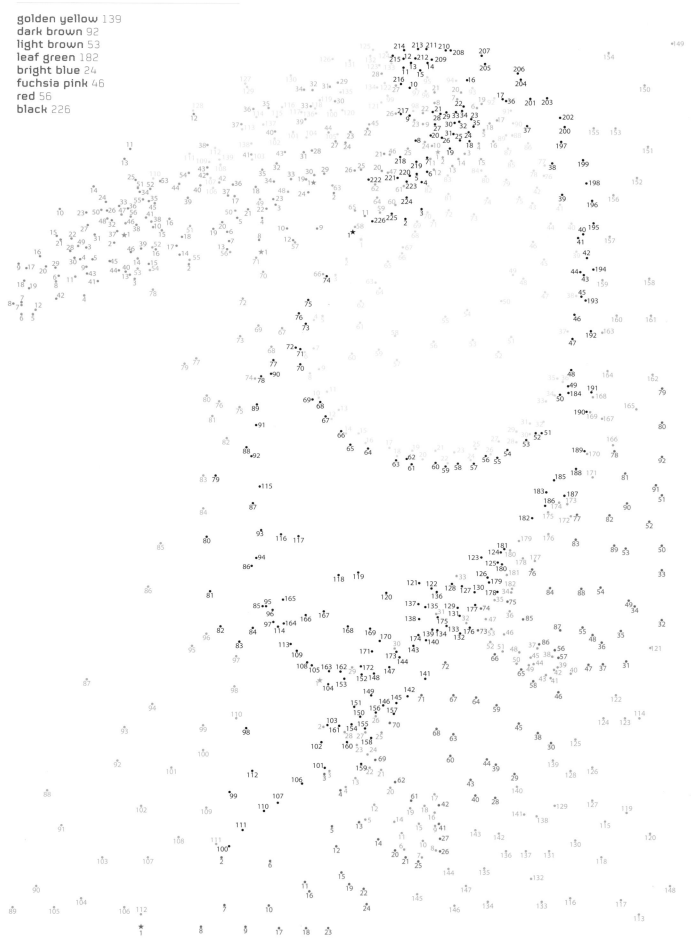

Frog Leap

ORDER OF COLOR SECTIONS

light orange	69	royal blue	144
leaf green	239	bright red	158
forest green	142	black	105

Chilled Turtle

ORDER OF COLOR SECTIONS

sea blue 48
teal green 231
warm gray 75

orange 89
dark brown 156
black 79

Vivid Gecko

ORDER OF COLOR SECTIONS

light green 185
pale brown 191
bright red 103

forest green 254
black 20

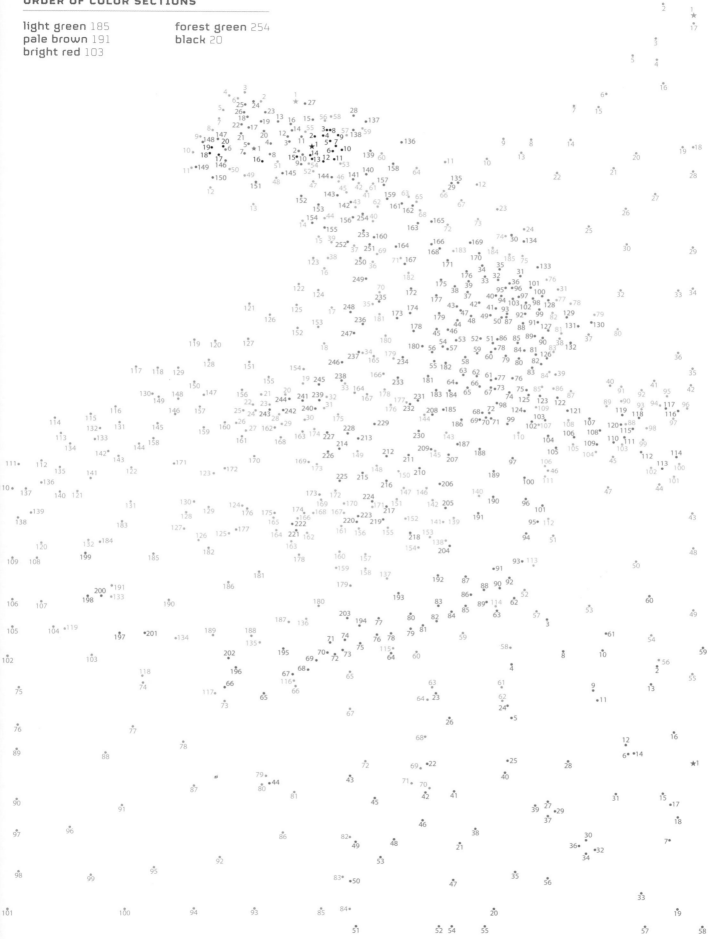

Delicate Dragonfly

ORDER OF COLOR SECTIONS

golden yellow 65   royal purple 75
bright blue 115   dark green 166
fuchsia pink 364   royal blue 146

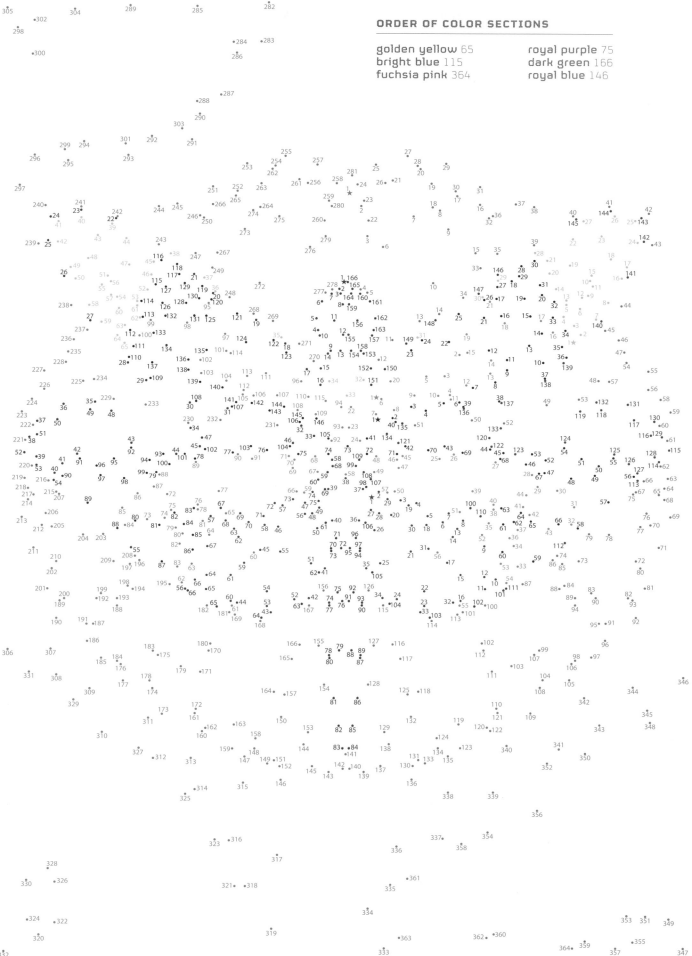

Clown Fish

ORDER OF COLOR SECTIONS

teal green 112
tangerine orange 178
fuchsia pink 263

burgundy red 197
black 245

Scuttling Crabs

ORDER OF COLOR SECTIONS

pale gray 134

golden yellow 69

pale orange 81

tangerine orange 274

steel gray 148

violet 35

burgundy red 148

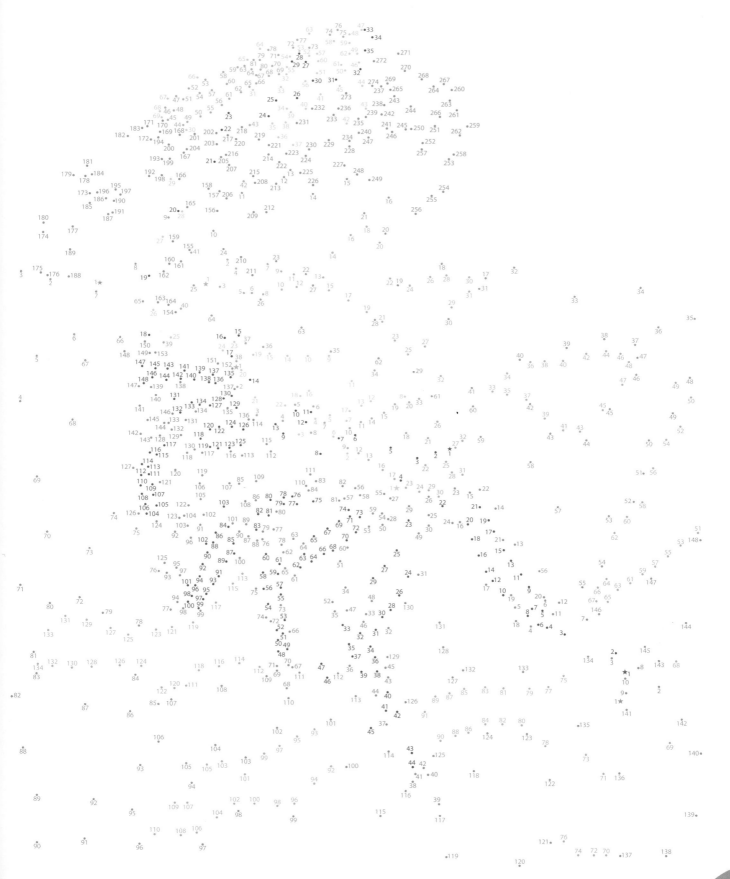

Face Off: Mandrill

ORDER OF COLOR SECTIONS

golden yellow 187   chocolate brown 179
bright blue 52   black 255
bright red 103

A Bloom of Jellyfish

ORDER OF COLOR SECTIONS

sea blue 66
teal green 79
light orange 131

tangerine orange 198
dusty pink 188
purple pink 250

Regal Ram

ORDER OF COLOR SECTIONS

orange 158   chocolate brown 381
soft gray 121   black 498
grass green 25

Hummingbird

Hummingbird

ORDER OF COLOR SECTIONS

green 127   fuchsia pink 64
royal blue 108   royal purple 192

Mandarin Duck

ORDER OF COLOR SECTIONS

light orange 249
green 354
fuchsia pink 73

bright red 58
chocolate brown 37
indigo blue 173

Prickly Hedgehog

ORDER OF COLOR SECTIONS

pale gray 106 chestnut brown 58
leaf green 164 dark brown 219
dark green 49 black 42

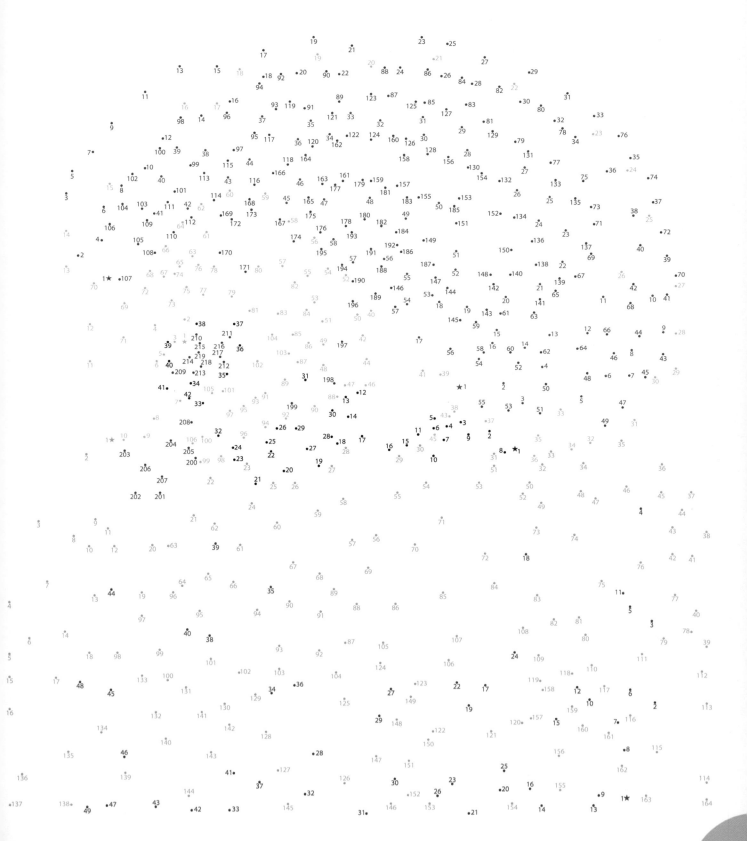

Colorful Bugs

ORDER OF COLOR SECTIONS

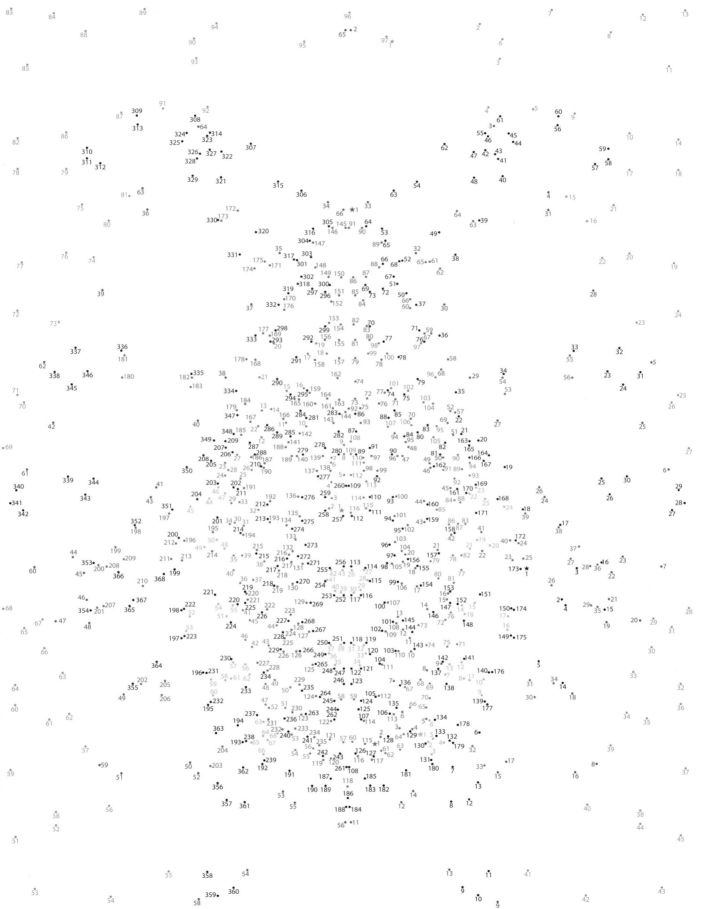

ORDER OF COLOR SECTIONS

pale pink 96   chocolate brown 187
caramel 398   black 176

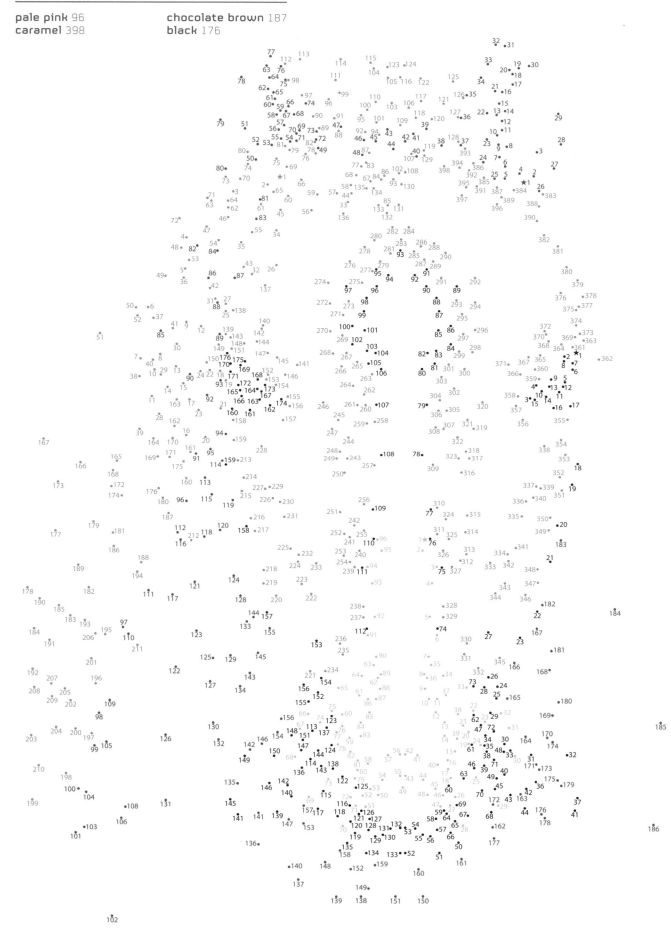

DOT-TO-DOT INDEX

Use the thumbnail images on the following pages to select the design you want to tackle next, or to help if you need any guidance when completing the puzzle.

Dawn Chorus

Coral Reef Critters

Lion's Roar

Macaws

Crowing Cockerel

Flutter Butterfly

Tiger Stripes

Flamingo Duo

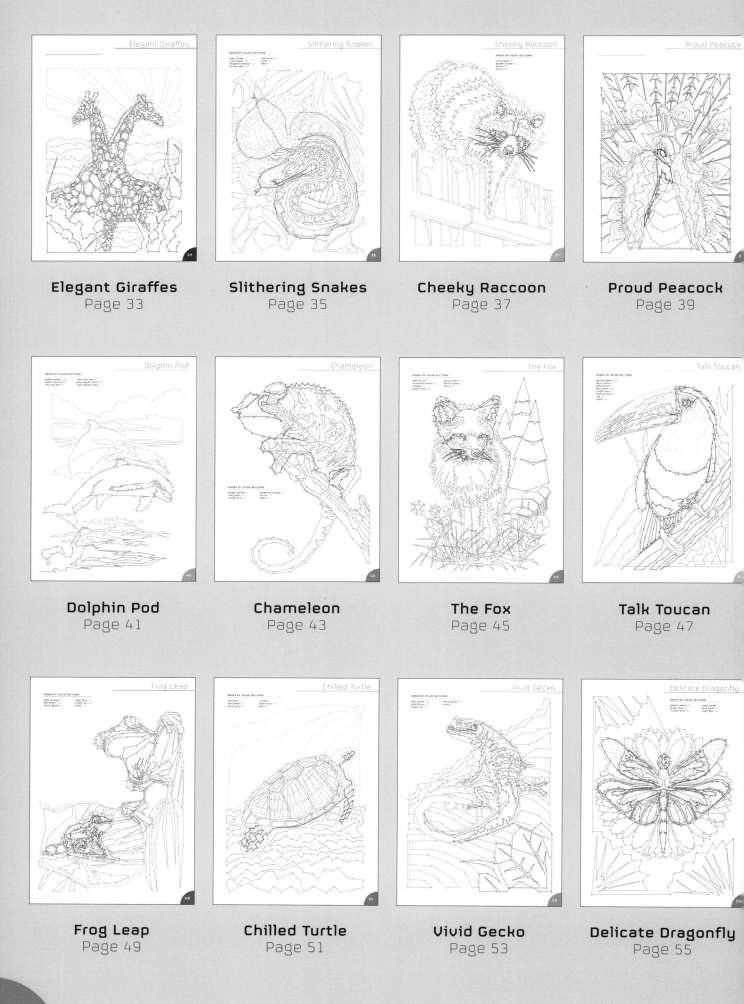

DOT-TO-DOT INDEX

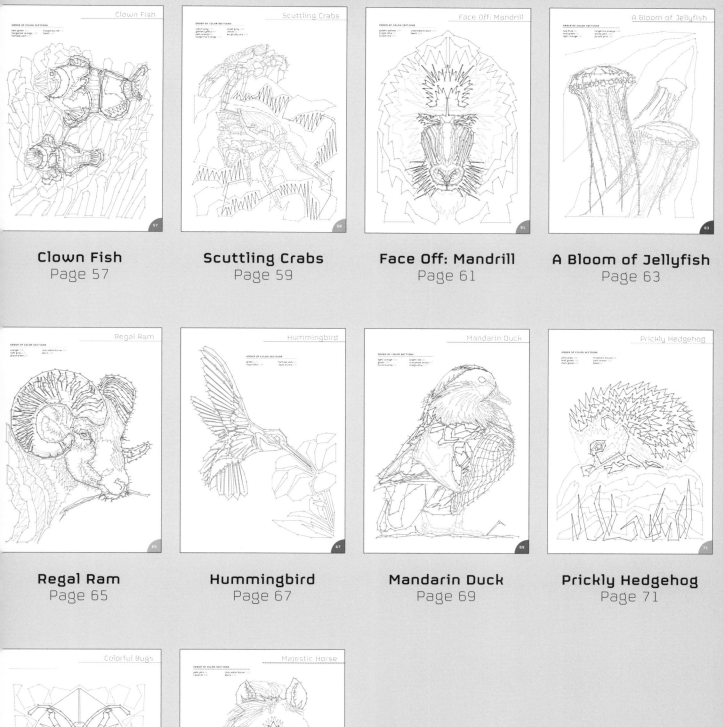

Acknowledgments

Quantum Books would like to thank the following for supplying images for inclusion in this book:

Shutterstock.com
Vichy Deal, page 9
Sonya illustration, page 13 (top left)
Pictures_for_You, page 13 (top center and right)
NattapolStudiO, page 13 (lower right)

Thanks to the following for their help in making this book:

To our fantastic illustrator Shane Madden, thank you for bringing this concept to life and producing such wonderful artwork. It has been great fun creating this riot of color with you.

To Emma Frith Suttey for her expert checking of all the puzzles and constant enthusiasm for the project.

Thanks also to Tilly Davis, Charlotte Frost, Emma Harverson, Nicky Hill, Tokiko Morishima, and Julia Shone for their editorial work; and to Mike Lebihan for the design work and cover design.